TUESDAY

Volume 7, 2013

Sandra Ellston and Ruth F. Harrison,
eds.

ACKNOWLEDGMENTS

Ellston's "On Seeing Li Bai in a Dream (after Du Fu)" is reprinted from *Poems Along the Way* (2012).

Esteve's "Sure," "Late Snow," "Snow and Starlight," and "A Declaration of Faith" are reprinted from *The Winter Sun* (2013). "Late Snow" was first published by *Fine Madness*, and "Sure" by *Hunger Mountain*.

Harrison's "*Arcos*: stones of the square" is reprinted from *Brevities*, Summer '07; "*Soliloquy*" from *Brevities*, No. 24, Feb 2005; "Closed and gone" from *Byline* 8/25/05; "Free horses: a *chansonette*" from *California Quarterly*, Vol. 33, No. 4, 2007; "Future Perfect, Yet How Intense" from *Mind in Motion*; "Watchers" from *Pen and Ink*, 2, Spring/Summer 1996, p. 11; "Dialogue among objects at dusk" from *Edgz*, Nov 2005; "Morning oasis: lean white moon" from *Edgz*, Fall 2005 ; "Another Part of the Forest," awarded 2nd place in the National Society of State Poetry Societies, first published in *Encore* 2002.

McGhee's two stories first appeared in "Voices and Stories" (2002, Xlibris) and again in 2011 through CreateSpace. "Stigmata" was also published in an edition of "The Portlander" from PSU.

Cover photograph by Rex Smith
Font, Book Antiqua 11
Anthology ©Turnstone Books of Oregon, 2013
©Individual authors retain copyrights of their works, 2013

CONTENTS

Tuesday Writers constitute the oldest continuous writer group in Lincoln County, Oregon, founded by Ruth F. Harrison in 1990 on the heels of a course she offered at our community college. The group is notable for its literary fellowship and the success of various members over the years as they complete projects, publish books, and win awards. This past year witnessed new books by members Patricia Ranzoni, *Flights and Glories*, Dorothy Black Crow Mack, *Anuk-Ite: Double-Face Woman*, Jean Esteve, *The Winter Sun*, Ruth Harrison, *West of 101*, and Sandra Ellston, *Poems Along the Way*. Kathleen Sullivan secured a New York literary agent, and Jean Esteve's previous book, *Off-Key*, was a finalist for the Oregon Book Award in poetry. Cynthia Jacobi won first place in the Members Only category in the Oregon Poetry Association contest this year.

Tuesday members have come and gone, but Ruth continues to anchor our group after these twenty-three years, and members respect her as our literary *eminence grise*. The group has met every Tuesday no matter what else is going on in the world; we met even on that fateful Tuesday of September 11, 2001. Participants have attended from along the entire Oregon seaboard, from Pacific City to the north to Florence to the south, and we have had seasonal members from Wisconsin and Maine. It is a diverse group, hearing both poetry and prose—mostly essays and memoir stories—from participants. Each year we acknowledge and celebrate our work in this anthology, currently volume 7.

In 2012-13, two members of the group for reasons rational only to them committed a crime against two other members. The issue was taken on by the district attorney, and the core group felt the imperative to move away from future threat. The Tuesday Writers moved to Thursday but retained their traditional name of Tuesday and their usual method of operation. This was a sad event for the group, and we mention it as a cautionary tale to sister groups: create an agreed-upon set of guidelines and be careful. We deem trust a vital element for a writers' group.

Current members of Tuesday include:

Ruth Harrison	Shirley Plummer
Brian Hanna	Kathleen Sullivan
Sandra Ellston	Donny King
Crystal McGuire	Orpha Barry
Sue McGhee	

And on occasion

Pat Ranzoni (from Maine)	Marcia Casey
Cynthia Jacobi	Jill Hardin (from Florence)
Fred Strauss	Carol Strauss
Jean Esteve	

Going Home

Orpha Barry

Afraid now of the going home
to the wrinkled faces and graying hair,
of companions whose once bright eyes
are tired and clouded
by unspeakable experience
in foreign lands.

Even afraid to weep
for so many already dead.
Are there ever enough tears?
Is there ever enough time
for the many who paid their taxes
and did their duties?

Afraid now to meet those
companions whose tears
trace the path back
to the bones of those dutiful
many who lie buried
in the genocidal dust,

under the fallen walls of
Jericho.

An Aroma of Earth

Orpha Barry

The day's sunlight has faded
by minuscule measure
bit by tiny bit retreated
into the weighty layer of fog bank.

The air becomes a gentle mist,
moist and quiet
consoling, consistent,
the color of ash.

The atmosphere thickens.
Within saturated air I inhale
odors of loam and sod and mold,
a fertile, earthbound bouquet.

Another breath, and I draw in
a deep, warm, vibrant fragrance.
I imagine the aroma of taproots and tubers
rhizomes and rootstock.

A cool whisper
of wind breathes
its own message
of approaching twilight.

With no sense of sunset,
I turn from the garden.

The old Maestro

Orpha Barry

Rivulets of sweat spill over pouches of heavy cheeks, then drip into the folds and creases between them to descend crossways down to chin, only to drop into the perfectly tied white bow, and onto the crisp pique of his waistcoat.

His clouded eyes, once piercing and demanding, blink back the salty sting, as his mouth opens slightly then widens in silent expression of the tones only the vibration of oboe reed can accomplish.

As his body twists and sways, his head trembles a little, a reminder of the many years this particular concerto has resonated to the mastery of his weathered baton that points and sweeps its way across the orchestra.

With his eyes tightly closed, and left hand fingers tapping the tempo on his chest, the baton begins to rise in anticipation of the final cord. An expression enraptured, transforms his weary countenance to one of sublime exaltation.

Once again his discerning insight has mastered the composition and he stands, dripping wet and trembling, between orchestra and audience. The hero of the hour and so many past, but how many, if any to come?

Moonrise

Orpha Barry

Having wandered down the years
to now, I linger in this place
absorbed in a pleasant ease,
resting here between the folds of time.

Empowered by beauty and birdsong,
the cliffs and shoreline
speak of eternal mysteries,
sing of nature's sacred principles.

Through the mist the moon rises,
a glowing lamp in the heavens
to guide the footsteps
of the foolish and the wise,

and those pretenders
who embrace their parts, assigned
by chance or design,
to wander their own lonely pathways.

Question

Orpha Barry

Is it worth anything,
all this love and duty,
the building of the fires,
the boiling of the soup
preparations for even
a solitary visitor?

Perhaps it is not the doing,
but the waiting,
just resting, as the tides change
as the rains clear,
to expose the distant sunset,
here at the center of it all.

Where meaning drifts on the tide
flowing in and out and in again
not grasping, but releasing
until all trace of us,
of our futile efforts is gone,

revealing the way beyond.

Hamlet Poems, A Voiced Sequence

Crystal Mc Guire

A Dead Man's Request
                    - Hamlet

In the middle of the moon's light,
you came to me like a dream
asking only one thing:
To avenge who made you
live out your time in purgatory.
I lightly took the challenge
as you left as quietly as
the night.

My heart was more lonely than before.

Mechanically Unstable
-Hamlet's stepfather, Claudius

His instincts were right,
as though right
were a destination
instead of a state of mind;
thoughts scampered through my head,
bolting concept to plan
like a well-oiled machine,
awaiting the key
to commence tragedy, hasty intentions.
The deadened belief inside me
had begun to operate on its own,
rotating gears, circulating wheels.
The notion
his father's world
would look better on me.

Peering In

-Hamlet's mother, Gertrude

You trespassed,
no matter how warranted
it was or should be.
I did not want a peeper
looking into my windows,
pulling the drapes of my secrets back
in hopes of revealing any truth inside.
I know what I am,
my reflection frail and warped
stained windows;
I spent years hanging over an open fire.
I see quite clearly
though you are an extension of me;
I will not bear the risk
to be unkept.
So no matter how much you knock on my door
or rap at my window,
I cannot really let you in.

Survivor

-Hamlet's friend, Horatio

As we were swept away
in the waves of venom,
tipped in goblets
and at the dull side of the sword,
battle ensued quickly
deafening the sight;
death taunted each of us.
I was able to sit back, regarding,
only able to live
with toxic memories,
relived by my own words.
I wish I could have saved you,
my friend, instead of only the tale.

Soaking Away My Sorrow
-Ophelia

The garlands I braided
were to lift the feelings of loss from the air.
The heavy clouds made it too hard to breathe,
sorrow forced its hand upon me, my answer was those
trophies.
A form I could understand, like *to sing* instead of *cry*.

Hinging them upon the willow, feelings to bedposts
before I lay me down. The loss has worn me down.
The soaking brook had gentle hands,
toiling at my hair and clothes like a mother's serene touch.

Madness

-Hamlet

I am Alice, if I were to be a woman
tumbling down the rabbit hole.
Upon my arrival,
I am lost of words and their meanings.
Primal as a wolf to its prey
hoping to find a cure for the hunger inside me.
I do not like this place, where mad is normal
and normal has eyes for vengeance.
I visit you, hair matted
like a tangled undergrowth
wanting a piece of the sky,
my shirt ajar, off hinged.
A door a few inches from being flush
at the bottom, never able to scrape
a perfect close. I had no time
to become such a stray in Wonderland.
All I had was you, Ophelia.
I searched for an exit from my cloud
of mourning in your eyes;
the only answer that surfaced was beauty.
There was no dream to awaken from.
I held your arm and nodded in agreement
desperate for a key that didn't exist.
Instead two people became misplaced within
the eyes of each other.

Last Thoughts
-Polonius

My intentions were not clean:
strings attached
such sufferings stretched to my
daughter's ache.

Against my estranged worry,
it transformed Claudius's plot,
and I hid to uncover the truth
of what it meant to be faulty.

Knowledge did not become a power
I wanted to possess
as demons possess more
than your mortal coil could contain.

Flesh to air, mind to suffer,
I can see you are less a man with a sword,
oppressed from scorns of patience barred
to be treated as wrong as your father.

My fate rested in your hands,
in my silence,
in your mother's room.

On Seeing Li Bai in a Dream (after Du Fu)

Sandra Ellston

When you departed, I wept.
Again and again we who remain
suffer sorrow and sorrows.
A miasma shrouds
the river of no return;
there I cannot seek news of your fate.
Yet here you are in a dream —
in my mind, your countenance clear!
What net can snag
a feather from your wing?
You pass a distant road
unafraid, your soul at peace.
You come to me through the deep green
maple woods; you disappear
slipping through the narrow
mountain pass at night.
All that's left is the moon
filling my house to the rafters.
Still I wonder where it is you wander.
The river is wide and deep,
the current strong.
If your crossing faltered,
were you prey to the king
of water monsters?

The Development

Sandra Ellston

Someone has brought in bulldozers.
They are clearing out the trees
in the swale along the creek,
between the water and the highway.
Now a fallen trunk rests
across a would-be road.
The otter and mink have fled.
We saw them crossing the drive
heading north, away from the creek,
eyes down-turned, determined.
Relics of prior attempts
to civilize this ground emerge,
a concrete pad, rusted pipe,
bottles. The earth remains marshy.
Finding a grand new pasture a boon,
deer show themselves, grazing.
At dusk I see a buck elk
at ease in the field.
My toes go cold with the damp
and I turn to higher ground.

In Dreams

Sandra Ellston

> *Eventually the day of judgment will dawn,*
> *when you realize that all life is a dream.*
> --Chuang Tzu

Today I slept 'til ten,
making an eleven-hour night.
My friends say they have trouble
falling asleep, staying asleep,
catching enough sleep to get by.
By day their eyes squint, glint
like shells hidden in ridges
of sand. They move slow
as stop-time and for them
the thrill is gone. They die to sleep.
Reality's too real.

My dream-life charges on.
Last night I wandered the halls
of a college again
trying to find my office
and knowing I was late for class.
One trip to the loo
and, episode two,
back at the dorm
I wake to remember
there's a final in a class
I always forgot to attend
and still can't find the room.

It's the American Civil War.
I've been entrusted with letters
from home, mail for soldiers.

I wander the fields
with my pack and names on a list—
but all I can see, a macabre crop of the slain.

I own an antique shop.
It's at the far end
of my enormous house,
room and room and room—
I seek to find its end—
finally down into cellars and tunnels
all filled with fine relics,
artifacts of domestic life, wardrobes
and china cabinets, chairs
and trestle tables,
the occasional coffee stand.
At the end a small door
opens, my shop door,
onto the street
and the soaring cathedral spire.
I dream this again and again.
The light out there makes me squint.

My man is still in bed—
his eyelids twitching, dreaming on.

The Season's Way

Sandra Ellston

Always, but especially
late afternoon
late summer
a something hangs in the air
like smoke from a burn barrel
and sidles into the mind.

Our slant of light
elusively changes
to let philosophy reign.

Even in a moment of here, now,
while I dead-head the last of the dahlias,
three questions take shape and haunt me
but mostly the last:

do we exist?
is the world real?
and how am I to live?

I take one more turn
'round the garden path
and pull up two more mole-weeds--
then return to my desk to try again
to write.

The Face of Evil

Sandra Ellston

My mother has always been a staunch and unquestioning Methodist, but considering theological questions is not in her nature. Once we were talking about evil in the world, and I asked her if she believed in the devil, a literal devil physically present and active on earth. Without pause she said, "Oh, yes."

I've seen evil in the eyes of humankind, certainly. If we include the whole array of deadly and venial sins, for me they glimmer forth sometimes upon first meeting a person. Something seems a bit askew, it makes me feel uneasy, and then there is that glint in the eye—of deception, of desire, of lust for power or advantage. These people seem slippery and instinctively to be avoided. It is always amazing when we hear about, say, a man who has kidnaped three women and kept them locked up in his house as sexual slaves for ten years without anyone catching on. When the neighbors say he was a quiet man who kept to himself, I wonder when their moral radar went on the blink.

We want to think well of others. We don't relish looking into the eyes of evil and this has made us, in many cases, all-accepting. We don't like to draw the line or turn in our neighbors. We're willing to accept a world of shades of grey. When does grey edge into black?

A friend told me a story about when she was working at a real estate kiosk just off I-5 near Albany, Oregon. It was visible from the freeway and completely isolated at the end of an entry road made just for the office.

. . .

One night near closing time a VW bug chugged up the road and parked and a handsome, charming man came in. He wanted to use the rest room, and then he plunked down to chat—about real estate, about anything. Her radar blipped. She told the man she was closing. She told him the manager would be there to help her close (a white lie). He remained seated, chatting away charmingly. She said his eyes were like those of a cobra, and it took all her will to resist. Finally, miraculously another car did pull down into the drive, and the charmer beat a hasty retreat. She noted his license number and reported it to the police. The visitor's name was Ted Bundy.

Another friend tells about attending a party in the 1960s in Oregon's Willamette Valley, where a wild-eyed man was recruiting young women for his commune. He singled her out and took her aside, persuasively arguing for a free-kind of religion if she would follow him. He was charismatic and exercised a magnetic pull—but his eyes carried a glimmer of a sadistic evil, and she drew away. His name was Charlie, and later she recognized him as the infamous Mr. Manson. It was the eyes in both cases that gave them away.

This is new-world evil, the realm of the serial killer. We have nearly become inured to its factuality, through crime fiction and crime-show media. "Law and Order" and "CSI" have made us all too aware of man's atrocities to other men. These days we are able to abide carnage and cannibalism, torture and sadism, through the buffering formula of the horror film. On any given evening, try reading through the plot summaries in the "Thriller" section of Netflix. The premise of every narrative will turn your blood cold. One would think we live in a nation of serial murderers.

* * *

In my twenties I went to a big-screen public theater to catch a new release, "The Exorcist." This to me is the most frightening movie of all time. It focuses on an innocent teenager who then is corrupted, body — and we hope not completely — soul, by a motiveless demon. Who has not played with a Ouija Board? In my teenage years I hosted a slumber party with several friends as guests, and we pulled out the board. The little pointer on the board sped around with alacrity. It spelled out sexual words and actually moved its pointy side right toward the crotch of one of the girls. We were alarmed. What had we broached? Our Craftsman house had enormous walk-in closets, so we went in there to conduct an experiment — could we summon a spirit?

We turned out the light and sat on the floor around a vanity bench with just our fingertips touching its top. Sure enough, the table lurched, and we ran out screaming. I threw the Ouija Board away after that and heard that it serves as an invitation to evil spirits. Teenage girls are allegedly specifically susceptible. "The Exorcist" was so horrible because of the corrupted face and especially eyes of the hapless teenage girl. When asleep, she looked sick but human. When her eyes opened, with the demon peering out, her evil was horrifying.

We look to Eastern Europe for ancient demons. This is the nesting spot for the vampire legend, and vampires have many cousins. In 1998 my husband Carl and I went on a tour of Vienna, Budapest, and Prague with his choral group, which had appointments to sing in various venues, mostly grand medieval cathedrals. Each of these capitals is glorious in its own way. When we first alit at the airport in Prague after midnight, I felt the old world vibration. Our tour guide solidified this impression, as she was a tall, slim figure with wild gray hair. Prague is especially fascinating because of the vibrancy of its old town area. People crowd into the plaza at night for the magic of the small lights illuminating the medieval square as the clock strikes, bringing forth its drama of classic characters, Death and deadly sins. One can walk the narrow streets for shops and concert halls and college buildings around every turn. And there is the famous Charles Bridge, a wide highway for pedestrians across the Vltava River.

Photo by Dana Shanburg

Here artists and artisans have set up their displays, from scarves to jewelry to carvings to paintings. One display caught my eye, as every painting was of the same subject, who was a demon. The cheeks were impishly round but ruddy and rather crusty-looking. There were small horns protruding from the mussed hair, just above the temples, and his tongue lolled. It was a hideous image because it combined a human playfulness with the animalistic, making it monstrous. The eyes concentrated this unsettling mix: recognizably a human relative but with an unworldly menace. Who would paint such an image, and repaint and repaint it? We were surrounded by the same face on many canvases.

I regret that these were the days before digital photography, for the painter and vendor sitting with his wares was . . . the demon himself! These were self-portraits! The man was precisely as he appeared in the paintings, but now we could also see that he was short in stature. I saw him. The shock and absurdity of the situation registered. He glanced my way, and with the gaze I felt chilled. I'm not sure I would have been able to summon the courage to pause, direct my attention toward him and his toward me, and take his portrait even if I'd had a good camera. We quickly walked away and briefly discussed what we had seen. None of us could make sense of it.

Was this a jokester wearing phony horns? They looked organic. Was it a man afflicted with tumors on his temples who had decided to make the best of it? Unlikely. Had we witnessed a real demon among us, on that medieval bridge in Prague? His face and gaze still haunt my dreams, and I've found that others have reproduced similar images. I wonder if my mother had it right all along. The devil can walk the earth and look us straight in the eye. I think I witnessed one of his manifestations.

From "Onibaba."

Who Has A Soul?

Kathleen Sullivan

In the mid 1960's I was a member of the Ursuline Sisters of Paola, Kansas, and my first assignment was to a grade school in Bartlesville, Oklahoma. The initial months of teaching thirty-four third-graders in an unair-conditioned classroom in the Oklahoma heat was exhausting. Each day after school, I walked into the cool convent, collapsed on the sofa for a half-hour or so and tried to regroup before eating supper, reviewing lesson plans, and grading papers. By Halloween, the temperature had dropped, and I had fit into a comfortable pattern with the classroom. I realized I wasn't temperamentally suited to be a primary school teacher; I had been a hyperactive child who had matured into a hyperactive adult. Someone calmer like Sister Mary Margaret who taught first grade was better suited, but I could manage the role with a moderate degree of success.

Our nation was torn by racial violence and the war in Viet Nam and at twenty-two I was restless to fill a larger role. One evening after supper, I asked Sister Marcella, our local superior, for permission to join the NAACP. Before I died, the world had to be to be a better place because I had walked upon it, so I needed to get busy.

"I didn't know there was a chapter here," she said.

"Yes, I called around and located them. They meet every Sunday at two o'clock."

She wasn't crazy about the idea, but she finally authorized it. When I began attending meetings I was the only white member while a large percentage of my fellow members were black ministers in and around Bartlesville. To Sister Marcella's dismay, I was invited to speak in their churches and did so on several occasions. After one speech a member came up, greeted me warmly, and told me that he was honored that I was there. We conversed for a while and he made a comment about my wonderful family. I was confused. Gradually I realized that my round Irish face and Irish surname had been fertile grounds for a rumor that I was related to the Kennedys. I had wondered why I was treated with such respect and high regard; I hated telling him we weren't related.

One Sunday afternoon there was an important first for Bartlesville: black and white ministers agreed to meet in order to try to avoid the outbursts of racial violence that were occurring in major cities throughout the United States. I was embarrassed that the Catholic pastor had declined my invitation.

We sat in a circle and had a frank, open discussion.
"Do you have any black members in your congregation?" I asked one of the white ministers. He looked at me with obvious surprise and shock.

"No," he said. He hesitated for a few minutes, and then added, "Our church has been debating whether we should allow blacks to become members of our congregation. That issue has not been resolved."

I was stunned. "Your church doesn't allow black members?"

"It's always been a tenet that we couldn't have black members. I've been trying to get that changed. I haven't had much success up to this point."

"How do you justify not allowing blacks to be members? How can you call yourselves Christians and refuse admittance to others?" I was filled with the righteous indignation and spotless clarity of youth and blind to the obvious fact that the man before me wanted to be part of the solution, not the problem.

He was quite embarrassed. He studied his feet, stretched them out in front of him, and then pulled them back. He looked up at me. "Until two years ago it was a tenet of our church that Negroes didn't have souls," he said.

The faces of the black ministers in the circle remained fixed and emotionless. Not a hint of surprise. I sat back as if slapped. Only persons with souls can be church members. Negroes have no souls. Therefore, Negroes could not be church members. It fit perfectly into the syllogism form that Sister Augustine had taught me in Logic class. I had never before understood how racial prejudice really worked. I was stunned.

"How do you define Negro?" I asked.

Startled, he looked around. "These good people."

"What of mixed marriages?"

"Anyone with Negroid blood is a Negro," he said.

*   *   *

I raised my left hand slightly and looked at the scar that had been formed by surgery when I was seven. The surgeon had been fascinated in my follow-up visit.

"The scar is a keloid," he said. "Only Negroes form keloids."

I told Grandma what the doctor said. "Am I a Negro, Grandma?"

Grandma was from Virginia and assured me that there were no Negroes in our woodpile. We didn't have a woodpile and if we did why would they be in it? Whatever it meant, I was not to mention it to anyone ever again in my life.

*   *   *

"Anyone with Negroid blood is a Negro?" I asked.

"Yes," the white minister said.

I looked down at my hand. Maybe. Who knew? "Well, for heaven's sake."

I wanted to ask if there was any possibility that, in accordance with his Church's teachings, he didn't have a soul, but I was gradually learning that some questions are better left unasked. I looked around the circle at the dark smiling faces of my brothers and sisters in Christ. That cliché took on new meaning.

The minister stared at me while I laughed.

Arcos: stones of the square

Ruth F. Harrison

Hawks cross and recross
the deeps below us. Various
people sitting. One, an old man,
perches on piled brownish slabs
of stone, a fence to mark
the boundary pause
between the placid plaza
and the deep. Olive groves, grayed
green, color the afternoon distances.
Spain's limpid sunlight wavers
on far fields of sunflowers
        a yellow mist
            the dust

Soliloquy

Ruth F. Harrison

on a superfluous
wednesday, shadows

lying limp in corners
pooling on the floor

I don't suppose
I'll die at all

why bother?
maybe the drama

but then, you
wouldn't get to observe

a fine line separates
dim spectators from

the spotlit fellow in
mid soliloquy.

Closed and gone

Ruth F. Harrison

The place where words live
lies deep in darkness. They've
closed the shutters and drawn
the shades. The *return at*
clockhands hang limp, flaccid.
I've tried the handle but
nothing turns. The garden
and pool are fenced and silent,
no access to footpath and
leafy shade, no feeding
the swans, the black one
the white one, no resting
at ease on the garden bench.

By day and by night there's
this arid grubbing to find
the lost ones, the vanished lambs
and never a trace where
they've wandered, cropping.
Browsing invisibly near at hand?
or gone from this place past
those pewter mountains--?

If anyone sees them, I've
posted rewards: Return
the herd for a brand new poem.
No questions asked and
no answers given, only the best
I can spin from straw.

Free Horses: *a chansonette*

Ruth F. Harrison

They raise a thunder on the blowing plain
pinto and sorrel, white, and black and bay
I hear their ghosts tonight in this chill rain
and marvel at their glorious array.

They raised a thunder on the blowing plain.
Their time is past, but how they lived their day:
to run was high delight, each wind-tossed mane
and tail wrote wildness on the sky, the way
pinto and sorrel, white, and roan and bay
understood life, unfettered. Wordless, sane.
Foals caper, tossing heads, they snort and neigh
and nicker near the creek, wild grass their grain—
I hear their ghosts tonight in this cool rain.
Their majesty is speed, their labor play—
I mourn their passing in my mind's bright pain
and wonder at life's rich variety.

They raise a thunder on the blowing plain
pinto and sorrel, white, and black and bay
I hear their ghosts tonight in this chill rain
and marvel at their glorious array.

Future Perfect, Yet How Intense

Ruth F. Harrison

We shall have arrived in the future
    at 9:23.
The flight may have been perceived as
  stimulating, the landing as silken
the limo and rental car timetables
  as eclectic—

We shall have been surrounded by it-- all of it--
   for eight minutes by 9:31.

  All, all will have assembled there, the helipads

 and jet-buggies, the air skis and cellophane
   wings, the lucite zithers and gamelans
areaways lined with buckets of cosmos,
   tubs of moonflower ...

For the occasion we shall have pierced our lips, be
    wearing studs of chrysoprase
   shall have plaited one tiny fashionable braid in
      our upright hair;
   designers
will have tied our hemline about one knee

Every person will have been happy for an hour and
   25 seconds.

Women, men will have been
  drinking cherry espressos, dipping
   chamomile hips in whipped brandy, the
    hors d'oeuvres ordered in serried rows, oh,

and

there will have been laughing and singing and
flashing of teeth, and
the outer darkness will have been declared a
mistake, will have been abolished by
unrescindable decree

and Lucifer blessed and forgiven, the
fallen angels redeemed
and reason and truth will have been seen to prevail
by 11:02 ....

Watchers

Ruth F. Harrison

Wake, for the hour has come to throw off sleep;
Some small flame glimmers in our soul's dark night.
We watch and wait for light across the deep

and though it isn't easy yet, to keep
a darklong vigil for some phantom sight,
we wake. The hour has come to throw off sleep.

In the black reaches of the night, some weep
wanting a solid word, a hope more bright—
and watch and wait for light across the deep.

We browse our lives like flocks of well-fed sheep
moving from field to fold, not conscious, quite
Wake! for the hour has come to throw off sleep.

There will be time hereafter for such sleep
as follows battle. Set your spirit bright
to watch and wait for light across the deep.

Our lives are lent us briefly, not to keep;
our chance to learn to soar is small and slight.
Wake! for the hour has come to throw off sleep
to watch and wait for light across the deep.

Dialogue among objects at dusk

Ruth F. Harrison

A Burger King cup, dragging the wind behind it,
skitters across the path.
They make a desolate sound, the wind
not wanting to go in dark and cold
the cup chatters, insists -- *come on, it's just a little
way, you're only young once, and free.*
The wind saying, *I was never young. I will never
be free. That* free-as-the-wind *stuff--that's for the birds.*
The cup saying *Come on ...come on. Fuddy duddy.*

The wind dragging its heels, whining ... *always
tied to something, can't move without stirring
something up ...* When the cup lets it go,
a newspaper latches onto the wind, clings
flapping: *You can't get away, whap, whap
swoosh.* Says the wind *Can't this wait until
morning?* The paper sneers. *I'm not a
morning paper, flop, flop.* Cats hide watching,
in doorways. They can read bare wind.

Morning oasis: lean white moon

Ruth F. Harrison

This morning the highway will not keep its distance
its sounds circle my remote small house like
camels caravaning around an oasis

but more like strangers
not meeting your eyes
parting around you on the sidewalk

Their *shhhhhh* is endless, they hush the earthsounds
come and are here and gone
and come again louder, smothering

finch calls, grass whispers,
a quail scoots, dog toenails.
Only the surf competes.

It reminds us *I am not so transient
as all that.* A lean white moon
watches the rising day.

Another Part of the Forest

Ruth F. Harrison

> I'll fetch you a dark lantern.
> —John Webster,
> > *The Duchess of Malfi,* V, iv, l. 44.

Lighting a path with darkness is an art
To find the unknown when the known way fails.
See how this dark ray picks direction out
In the flat blaze of noon, when insight's dead
And then, consider how the light is fled.

Something of blindness guides our Webster's quill
Throughout *Malfi.* Those deeds done in the dark
Lead on to dark, and darken in inverse
Proportion to the efforts to shed light—
Like light in burglars' lanterns, wit's encased
To present one small beam so focused that
The playwright's lost himself and barked his shin.
How else explain how word led on to word
To give a sycophant these dying lines
(In action where the cast of villains all
Are men, or are such replicas as had
Justified Plato's ban on theatre—
Wherein the sole strong character is she
Who died so young she dazzled, and whose sin
Was this: she stooped to love a decent man):

In what a shadow, or deep pit of darkness,
Doth womanish and fearful mankind live ...

Moans vile Bosola, who, to keep his job,
Abetted and committed crime on crime—
Brandished his noose to frighten and appall

* * *

Her who had funded him, who was his friend
Until he stole her years and left her dead.
Let us pass by her brothers, wealthy, strong,
Who made themselves her keepers to one end,
That they might slander her and take the life
Of her young family to secure the place
Her birth had granted her. Well, as you see:
To show men cruel, grasping, scheming, and
As envious rivals, murderous to their trust,
Then name them *womanish* for their manly deeds
Seems irony beyond my power to write.
Were definition based on these five acts
We'd redefine the slandered word to mean
Playful, brave-hearted, loving, generous,
Trustful, and *capable:* for Webster proves
His duchess and her handmaid, deed and word,
To fit these terms. By definition, then,
That's *womanish.* And these terms are no part
Of what Bosola means with line one-ten.

I'd swear the tailor's son wrote this at speed
Borrowing rhythms from a dying bard,*
Failed to reread and blotted not a word
Before he shipped it off for patronage
To Baron Berkeley, wooed with subtler lines
Of flattery to his lordship's noble mind
Than any subtlety within the play.

All this one might condone, and sift for gold
Each sentence, and ignore the dross, and praise
The writer for his vigor, for that *dark*
Prevailing— yes, pervading every Act—
These I concede. And yet I will maintain:

Though he's John Webster, it's a blindfold pen
Writes *womanish* to dispraise the deeds of men.

Give and Take

Shirley Plummer

Give me back those two and a half inches
and the twenty pounds to fill them out
so that my skin does not drape
like one of those wrinkled dogs,
creature in a cloak too big

Alternatively, send me the tailor
who can take up the seams
and shorten my own too big cloak

Not only does gravity drag me down
but I have shrunk
inside my blanket of skin and flesh
which now must settle around
what is left of me

Oh, give me back my pinkness and suppleness
and, when fate catches up with me
cut me off suddenly in the flowering of my age

. . .

signs

Shirley Plummer

You tramped carelessly past the warning signs
I was angry that you smashed across my field of flowers
But you put your hands on my waist and lifted me high
Swinging me around, and I was surprised into laughing

You said exciting things I had never heard
You did entrancing things I had never done
my self faded into it and my world changed
it became strange — mysterious — enchanted

The dark-eyed boy danced before he walked
we three danced through gardens and fields and woods
though you often went away during the day —
One day you did not return

For years the two of us danced inside and out
laughed through wood and garden and house.
Years later the man came back —
but — only to take the boy away

I shattered — pieces fell to the ground
a broken nest and shells — all empty
alone in a trampled, unkempt field of flowers
I was nothing and could not return to what I had been

Promises

Shirley Plummer

I stumble on an earth turned quaking bog
and find no mooring

you held me next your heart while you had heart to love
you bathed my eyes with gauzy light
you melted my flesh with waves of heat

you held me and I could not loose myself
you drowned me and I could not swim
you held me so near I only felt your heartbeat

you brushed my ear with whispering lips
my nape with softly touching fingertips
and your tongue tasted my skin

your ears heard my moans and cries —
and you promised all these would continue . . .
you promised . . . but now —

only half my wounded, aching self
shivers on the quivering earth
where I no anchor find

if only you had promised my leaving would be first

if only you had held the door . . .

Perhaps

Shirley Plummer

she did not lay herself down
on the flowing water
bedecked with flowers

she was face-down a-float
bumping over pebbles, slowing in the shallows
later she will wash swiftly
down the deepening river
unless
tangled in the reeds
or caught in a backwash
where
she will dismay the finders
who
could not know
that she would prefer being pushed
into the current
to continue on
to the sea

• • •

Legacy

Shirley Plummer

Gentle pleasures remembered . . .
smiles for some certain memories —
teasing after showers
for drying every toe —

some for remembrance,
of past feelings
of well-being entire

Longing sets in,
singular memories
bring sadder smiles

Tears spring recalling
skin touching skin
and later, warmth remembered
that recall can no longer feel

Remain
a winter nijuin

Shirley Plummer with Shirley Sachiko Kishiyama

fifteen years between
two infants with one name
born into the cold

certainly fortuitous
music from the crashing waves

drums and cymbals
echo of the firs cry
seabirds calling

inner ear of frozen bones
cannot hear the warning

above the temple bell
red leaves fall from the moon
painting the ground

water against the sand
always changing yet the same

under vine maple
gray haired lovers
holding hands

as the toddler makes her way
parents help her take a leap

• • •

new generation
journeys the uphill trails
large cobblestones

Amanda's tears cut a path
coast range of Yachats

hot winds blow away
leaves   muddy footprints   dried blood
old stories

longer nights
time slows to keep pace
each warms the other's hands

thin fingers intertwining
hold a cup with no handle

quilt around your back
huddling near the hibachi
room for another

the long gray shawl
her kindness

dance up the mountain
live   work   love   with laughter
walk down smiling

gentle rain in the meadow
shoes soaked on the way back home

● ● ●

forsythia
blooms first this year
a yellow spring

new green   joy   sadness
all remain unnamed

so bright
the daffodils
at noon, by eve we drooped
why did I cut
so soon

Conversations that Matter

Brian Hanna

My wife invited a bunch of people round to our house for what she likes to call Conversations that Matter. The guest list reflected as wide a political spectrum as would fit in our living room .Tongues were loosened by my supply of Two Buck Chuck that one guest felt obliged to inform the gathering actually costs $2.49 a bottle at Trader Joe's. A pattern soon emerged: Global Warming, Corporate Greed, and an activist Supreme Court were all taken to task, the latter for the presumption that corporations had all the same rights as people, and that politicians of every stripe were like villains, to be hissed off our little stage and into the wings.

Since the sound of ocean surf could be heard through our open windows, I introduced the topic of fish. Assuming the role of moderator, I put the question to the group: "Since a wild salmon cost about twice as much as one raised on a farm, should salmon therefore be consumed ONLY by those wealthy enough to go for the good (expensive) stuff? What of the need of those on a fixed budget or worse still, food stamps, for a piece of salmon that they could still afford? They wouldn't have time to catch a wild one for themselves, being, presumably, too busy looking for work.

I was surprised that even the most egalitarian among us held out against fish farms for that they would generate an alarming list of diseases that could be caught, during unprotected sex, by a Monarch of the deep from an adventurous "farm" girl who might have escaped into the ocean.

. . .

Tempers had become short, and a lady known for peace activism, if not for frivolity, was heard to say that that she should rather starve than eat farm salmon. I think she actually meant that everybody could starve before she would let them eat the farm fish. Someone asked if she could tell the difference in a blind taste test. She riposted gamely, I thought, that her principles would NOT allow her to submit to ANY test that allowed ANY farm raised fish into her mouth. Period.

Starvation in Africa was mentioned; that was clearly the cue for a pair of ample vegetarians, who seemed frankly more likely to succumb to obesity than malnutrition, to raise the question of the large amount of land required to raise beef compared to a much smaller amount, like one's back garden, that would keep you supplied with roots and berries. "We eat nothing with a face," they said firmly. "What about a head?" said someone, "or is cabbage out too?"

"Screw cabbage," I piped up. "What about sausages?"

"Try a veggie burger," the wife shot back. "Since your palette has become blunted with this two-buck chuck, you won't know the difference." It seems that a diet of vegetables can breed aggression just as readily as one that includes meat.

A reliable liberal voice changed the subject. "'Was it fair," he asked, "that a solitary youngster caught climbing out of your basement window clutching your flat screen TV could spend more time behind bars than a battalion of stock manipulators whose entrepreneurial activities had brought the economy to its knees.? Was the kid not simply practicing a more modest and less harmful version of 'entrepreneurial activity'?" That was too much for a

• • •

Republican whom I had always seen as a rather soft touch-
-though he does have a general tendency to ascribe
poverty to "inappropriate life style choices," a phrase he
currently uses a great deal.

"That's not entrepreneurial activity; that is crime!" he
said firmly. "I know crime when I see it." I wondered if he
really did but decided not to say anything.

At this point I sensed it was all getting too theoretical
and that we needed some stories. "How had we faced
hard times in our own lives? Had we experienced only
affluence or had we known scarcity as well? If so, how had
we dealt with it?" There were three people from the deep
south of whom I am particularly fond as they are always
upbeat. One, an ordained minister, told of parental
beatings but quickly moved on to a tale of sharing stone
soup with her neighbors. It was not just, I was relieved to
discover, a rock in a pot. It was a communal dish: some
brought a carrot or two and someone a cabbage, maybe a
turkey buzzard that had flown into the sights of some
sharpshooter. Everybody had a gun apparently. The point
was it was a chance to have a party. When the convivial
stone soup started to pall, there were always catfish in the
local pond.

A husband and wife from the same part of the States
told of going to the school prom together. They were
childhood sweethearts apparently. What did she wear?
Her mother, a resourceful woman, obviously, borrowed a
dress pattern from her neighbor and begged some empty
flour bags from a kindly grocer, then ran up a dress for her
daughter incorporating the advertising slogan on the sack,
which read (my friend wiped her eyes, at the memory)
THE FINEST FLOUR. It had continued, "'that Money can
buy," but her Mother had cut that bit out since it sent the

wrong message. Her beau that evening, now her husband of many years, beamed affectionately at her and announced gallantly, "She always looked good in the sack."

It was time then to hear from a lady with memories of wartime Europe and the bombing of her ancient capital by the allies, who were attempting to dislodge the Germans. There were food shortages and certainly no milk. Thinking that we had now reached rock bottom, and in an attempt to be supportive, I said, "Now surely that is truly as bad as it can get?"

Wrong again--but for two surprising reasons, the first that she experienced the air raid shelter as a particularly jolly place and secondly she was allergic to milk. "We were happy," she said. "We were all in it together, and I was lactose intolerant anyway."

It was at that point that I realized that Americans and those that live among them are deeply committed to the ethos of triumph over adversity. I had always thought that it was Reach for the Top in these here parts, but in fact it's more like a Race to the Bottom, in which the winner endures more setbacks and privations than his rivals, fights back against huge odds, and then and only then the hero gets the girl (or recently sometimes the guy) and they ride off into the sunset to enjoy whatever bliss their imaginations can contrive.

Our youngest member, who had been silent for most of the evening, was asked, by one of us wanting to involve him in the conversation, to reflect on Drugs, or if he preferred, The Cultural Differences between Islam and Christianity, a subject he was apparently studying at Community College. I admired his succinct answer that seemed to address both questions at the same time: "With Islam you generally get stoned AFTER adultery; with Christianity usually BEFORE."

I detected a certain familiarity in the pattern that our evening followed. We all seemed to subscribe to the notion that facing challenges was crucial to building character. I wondered dreamily where had I encountered the notion before, for it was getting late.

Ah, yes, that famous sketch from the Monty Python concert for Oxfam at the Hollywood Bowl: "The Secret Policeman's Other Ball." In it, you may remember, after a huge dinner a bunch of bloated celebrities are holding forth about their early struggles. It went, in part, something like this:

"I tell you," said the first, lighting a fine Havana. "When I was a child we were so poor my parents and us five children lived in a shoebox on the Interstate Highway. Every morning we would get up at 4 a.m., clean the highways with our tongues, and go off to work down the mines for ten cents a day." After a pause long enough to inhale the fumes of a fine brandy, another interjects, "A shoe box, eh?. . . .Luxury. . . there were a hundred and fifty of us and we lived in a rolled up newspaper in a septic tank."

I didn't share this with the group, as people who take suffering really seriously are often quick to suspect they are being laughed at.

Old Country Song

Donny King

Heartbreaks and cheatin' and total mistreatin'--
I'm tired of misleadin' you.
Cryin' and whinin' and double-two-timin'--
I'm tired of making you blue.

When I'm whipped and I'm beaten an' tired of my cheatin'
I remember who I'm doin' wrong.
Then I sip on my beer an' I wince back a tear
an' I feel like an old country song.

CHORUS:
Like an oh-oh-old country song
that's been on the jukebox too long;
its cryin' and whinin' makes me feel like dyin'--
I feel like an' old country song.

She played me and made me cry like a baby,
another sugar-daddy fool.
Cryin' and whinin' 'bout her husband's two-timin'
an' her boyfriend that's making her blue.

But I don't blame her, 'cause I tried to tame her
when I should have been aching for you.
Now I'm whipped and I'm beaten and tired of my cheatin'
an' I feel like an old country song.

CHORUS:
Like an oh-oh-old country song
that's been on the jukebox too long;
its cryin' and whinin' makes me feel like dyin'--
I feel like an old country song.

Like an oh-oh-old country song
that's been on the jukebox too long;
its cryin' and whinin' makes me feel like dyin'--
I feel like an old country song.

ADÓNDE VAS, MORENA?

Donny King

I try to pretend
My world didn't end
Pretend that the sky didn't fall

I try to pretend
You're still my best friend
I waited all day for your call.

CHORUS:
Adónde vas, Morena?
Morena, adónde vas?
Te necesito, Morena,
Morena, adónde vas?
Adónde vas?

Tu – me corazón,
Y when I'm alone,
I'm dreaming *solo siempre a ti.*

Aquí in my heart,
We're never apart,
I'm dreaming *solo siempre a ti.*

CHORUS:
Adónde vas, Morena?
Morena, adónde vas?
Te necesito, Morena,
Morena, adónde vas?
Adónde vas?

Family Style

Cynthia Jacobi

Pottery bowls squatted full on the table
Jane's paisley cloth under their warm rounded bottoms
Grandma's Japanese trivet gripped the gravy boat
dishes were passed to the left
Uncle Jim and his two boys dove into the noodles
    out of turn as expected
opinions wove into gossip
    topics forbidden were salaries, Grandpa's will,
    or the whereabouts of our cousin Paul
although they could be kind and generous
    this family had no culture for words of love
little ones did not hear
    good night I love you sweet precious
and so did not know
how to speak love later to their own
this family cheerfully nattered on
    speculating endlessly –
    who went where and when and why
    who should sweep their own alleys
    why Katzie married Ted with no hope of
    her own child since Ted had suffered mumps
    causing undescended testicles
but they did not speak of love

One Itch or Another

Cynthia Jacobi

My left ear itches.
My feet wriggle.
My hips shift.
I swallow – my tongue clicks.
I take a deep breath,
expanding elastic borders.
I furrow my brow.
Adjust my sleeve.
I place hand to cheek and lean in.
I look up.
I itch to get going.

Shakespeare Community Theater at Café Mundo

Cynthia Jacobi

1. Teatro Mundo

At outside performance in light mist at dusk
we sat on wood benches atop folded blankets,
my hair dusted with tree flakes loosened by
an actor's child perched overhead in the myrtle.
She watched her father and mouthed his lines.
The tarted-up Hussy in fur over satin works
for the tax assessor. A marine scientist
became the drooling, dull-witted Lout.
The three Generals: a baker, a social worker,
a popcorn vendor. What would we be
if we could choose yet again? A musical duo
played the only two songs they knew, viola
and accordion vibrating with passion. The play
commenced under open sky as couples
shared rice bowls, others drank beer. More
gathered 'round a fire pit, listening, intent.
Actors circled the courtyard perimeter speaking
over passing motorcycles and dog barks, their
feet crunching gravel behind the last chair row.

2. Umatilla, Two Rivers Correctional Institution

Inmates silent, absorbed by imported drama.
They see real fleshed breathing women.
They find men being noble - or not –

their actions impossible to undo
pain in their hearts exposed
minds wondering when and how -
asking that eternal question:
why am I here?

Telephone Connection: Information Please

Cynthia Jacobi

I leave a silent spot for you to place
an answer, to make some response
I comment about weather here
health of your pet
your aged electric fuse box
brakes on your car
Easy responses, one would think -
not too personal, not too demanding
The pauses grow longer
Still I leave the space for you to fill
The flow of words starts   halts   starts
You begin with local weather
Your dog threw up bird feathers
The repair bill was only $59
The brakes still grip

You planted the Japanese Maple

Then I know your day went well
That your dog sleeps at your side
That you want to live

Lost

Sue Mc Ghee

My breath is labored but I ski diligently down the hill. The wind whistles past my ears and I feel the tender pat of snow on my face. It is late afternoon and I am cold, but he is here. I feel him. I listen for his voice.

I fall, spread-eagle, skis askew, spraying snow in all directions. I am light-headed but I rise to my elbow and wait. My head clears but I have lost my goggles from the concussion of the fall. Without sun, there are no shadows; without goggles, there is no depth perception—everything appears flat. I stand, helpless and stunned and look overhead: roiling sky and furious snow. My body feels old and abused and I cannot decide which way to go. Below, stragglers scurry towards the bottom of the mountain like frightened animals searching for shelter.

How long has it been, I try to remember, since I waved to the excited tourists swinging overhead on the last chair lift?

"A ten year old," I called. "Look for a lost boy." My throat still throbs from the yelling. They leaned forward, straining to hear with knitted brows and good intentions, then looked ahead expectantly to the "Tips Up" sign and prepared to unload. An hour. It's been an hour.

I plunk one ski down and re-secure the bindings. I squint and widen my eyes. I can feel little droplets of ice adhere to the fine hairs around my mouth. I lick them and think of snow cones.

* * *

59

I hear Jason say, "Mom, I'm here, in the shack, that old shack, remember? I'm here.
Not too far. Remember, Mom?"

I feel my heart pulsing strongly; it shudders, then waits—a little wary of recent events. Perhaps it is grieving prematurely, I think. I imagine drops of red as it resumes its ancient beat. It is not too late. It is not too late.

"Listen, Bird," I hear from deep inside.

A shelter of trees looms before me. I ski towards the trees. It is dark here and I blink to adjust my vision. I want to linger where it is safe. I want to think of Jason.

"Bird," his dad said. "Watch those boys ski, now. See how loose they are? How graceful? They're not all tight and stiff, you see." And it was true. As tykes, they swooshed down the mountain on either side of me, like new born comets blazing sky trails. "They're in control though, Birdie."

And they were, of course. They were his sons, so they learned well the first time. And when Jason came to us late in life, he learned from them, his brothers. He took his place among them, with the confidence of the favored, which he had been by them as much as by us.

"Mom?" I swing around and almost lose my balance. Ritchie stands before me in this dark region of the trees. He is anxious and breathes hard. He holds a red ski parka out for my inspection. "Is this his jacket?" I shake my head. My voice is gone from the calling. There are new crevasses in my child's face, extending from either side of his nose down to the corners of his mouth, and deep horizontal lines above the eyes; his virgin beard is threaded with ice. I reach for his shoulder and squeeze him, my youngest, next to Jason.

"It's no one's fault, Ritchie," I say.

"He's a mountaineer, Mom. Don't worry. He and Dad knew this mountain better than any of us; remember when Jason was little and the two of them used to go out together when the rest of us were in school? He'll be alright. We'll find him."

"Of course. I know that!" But I sound cross, doubtful.

"The ski patrol is on the way up. They want everyone off the mountain, though."

I nod. We both look at the sky overhead and know that soon it will be too late.

"Are you okay Mom? You look beat. Do you want to start down?"

I shake my head again. I can see myself through the eyes of my son: tired and old, but a willful woman whose dead husband's words of encouragement live on inside of her.

"Bird, you can do it. You can have this mid-life baby. I'll be with you all the way." He lied. I had the baby and now he's gone.

Still, I listen. I try to remember. A cabin, years ago - - long before Jason, before the others. It was spring, and we had skied all day until our skin was parched from the blistering wind and our bodies ached for food and love. We slowed, and when our shadows grew large, painted by the sinking sun to the west, Charles stopped suddenly, spraying snow in a showy arc and gestured downward with his pole. As I approached the crest of the hill, I could see a little cabin, a shack, settled cozily in the deep drifts, its sturdy chimney barely peeping over the tops. The memory is soft and warm and it calms me. It was long ago, before the boys, long before Jason — just Charles and me and a warm night of love, a small cabin tucked away from the world, with neat stacks of wood and woolen blankets piled high on top of the rickety bed. We talked of it for many years. Then it faded, as memories do. And now it is like a patch of blue in a sky full of clouds.

The snow is fresh here beneath the trees and I must lean back on my heels to keep from sinking the tips into the powder. I think of Jason and the joy he gives me. This unplanned, untamed child, his father's seed. He is like the butterfly, wild and unpredictable — the elusive butterfly that appears late in season. I reject this unsought metaphor and fill my mind with the longing. My shriveled heart renews itself and pumps blood to restore my brain. I want to cry. I want to shout. But I must think!

A ten year old is lost and alone; he is a skilled skier, an avid mountaineer, an apprentice to the wild.

"He's strong, Birdie, and smart. He keeps up with the others already. Jason!" he shouted, " . . . keep those knees together!"

I see them in my mind, the four boys and Charles, schuss-bombing down the mountain. Five dark heads that bob in the distance like shining pieces of coal, innocent of caps, with thick black hair battling the winds and capturing the sun.

"Come on, Bird, take this last run with us." In my mind, he waves and laughs at my hesitation. He is a tall man, finely crafted, with broad shoulders and narrow hips. He is fiercely proud of his sons, all born in his country, all Colorado natives.

Jason says, "The cabin, Mom. I'm waiting."

Ritch shifts on his skis, positioning himself sideways on the slope. We have come from the trees and stand on "Nordic Face," a run we have all skied many times. There are no cabins, no shacks on this mountain, I am sure. Still I listen . . .

"Listen, Birdie. Listen to Jason . . ."

A cabin, somewhere. "Ritch," I shout, ". . . a cabin on this mountain?"

"What?" The wind bends the trees on the side of the run, their branches sweeping the slopes, and it stirs the powdered snow into furious eddies. Rich cups his hand behind his ear and yells. "What are you saying, Mom?"

". . . an old cabin; an old abandoned shack?" I shout above the storm, but my voice is thin and raspy. Ritch shakes his head in bewilderment, his eyes so wide I want to laugh. I feel like laughing suddenly and my chest expands. Yes, it's here, I know! I motion Ritchie to follow and I turn and point my skis downward. I remember to plant my poles to clear the moguls: "Good girl, Birdie! Plant those poles. Plant! Watch that bump!"

We fly down the hill, the wind at our backs. I am unexpectedly light, competent, but I tire quickly. Ritch takes the lead. He reads my mind: it is difficult to see and

● ● ●

it will soon be dark. We slow as he guides us through another cluster of trees, taking our time to reach the other side. For a moment, I think I cannot go on. My body rebels and I must catch my breath, but we parallel through the dark sanctuary of the trees until we are suddenly clear of them, then start down again. The wind is relentless; it is at our backs and out of the west. There is no one in sight. The ski patrol will not come until later, I think; the storm is too sudden.

Somewhere ahead, Ritchie disappears into a whirlwind of snow. I see nothing but dancing white. It is beautiful and frightening and I do not linger. I continue more slowly now, as the snow gathers quickly on my lashes.

"Mom. Over here." I stop suddenly and wipe the moisture from my eyes with my wet sleeve. My breath comes in spurts and I take time to position myself sideways at the top of a hill. I barely see Ritchie atop a small knoll twenty feet away. He waves at me with his pole. It is a triumphant gesture. But first I must slide down then painfully sidestep my way to the top of the knoll. I squint through an insistent vale of white.

It is there: a small shack, a warming cabin down the hill and to our right, barely visible from where we stand, but there, nestled in winter's prolific accumulation. It is appropriate -- shy and unassuming, but smoke rises stubbornly from an ancient chimney and is whipped and dissipated by the winds.

I look at Ritchie and my lips convulse to form a smile. He leans forward, gently touching my face with an ice encrusted mitten. Blood is pounding at my temples. He points thumbs up and laughs out loud. It is his father's

• • •

laugh and I am suddenly giddy. He plunks one ski down with a loud plop and then the other, releasing impacted snow glued to the bottom. He waits until my breath returns then points his skis down towards the shack. He glances back at me. Yes! I am ready!

I follow my son down the hill.

STIGMATA

Sue Mc Ghee

Carmelita!

IN THE NAME OF THE FATHER AND OF THE SON AND OF THE HOLY SPIRIT. AMEN.

Carmelita!

I WILL GO TO THE ALTAR OF GOD, THE GOD OF MY GLADNESS AND JOY.

Carmelita is a murderer!

I CONFESS TO ALMIGHTY GOD, TO BLESSED MICHAEL THE ARCHANGEL, THAT I HAVE SINNED EXCEEDINGLY IN THOUGHT, she strikes her breast, **WORD,** she strikes her breast, **AND DEED.** She pauses and strikes her breast a third time.

They drove her blindfolded to a warehouse on the outskirts of town, dragged her inside and threw her on the gritty concrete floor. They tied her hands behind her back and gagged her. The first one, thick and foul-smelling, plowed her ceaselessly, the second finally pulling him off that he could have his turn. After the third one rolled away from her, limp and whimpering his shame, they removed the gag: she had no strength to scream, they knew. The fourth cursed the blood which had begun to flow. The fifth slapped her hard across the mouth because there was no fight left in her. The salty, rust taste of blood trickled through her clenched lips and she turned her head to the side, knowing that she was going to vomit. Her mind, poised on the edge of the void, gradually slipped into it, sinking . . .

● ● ●

LORD HAVE MERCY.

CHRIST HAVE MERCY.

LORD HAVE MERCY.

When she awoke, someone was stroking her cheek with a damp cloth and sobbing. Her eyes were swollen shut and she could not see, but his touch was gentle. She sank into blackness again and when she regained consciousness, she found herself surrounded by the cleansing world of a hospital.

GLORY BE TO GOD IN THE HIGHEST AND ON EARTH, PEACE TO MEN OF GOOD WILL.

She stands, her gnarled hands grasp the splintered railing. She shuffles forward and bows her head. Her eyes, though, dart quickly from side to side.

Back then, back in the lean-bellied thirties, they did not speak of it. They did not speak of such things in this small, west Texas town of whirling red-brown dirt, where the dust comes and covers everything, even forgotten horrors and hate and ignorance and self-righteousness.

They never found the perpetrators.

"Must have blown in from the north with all the rest of the dirt we've been getting," the sheriff had said. "Then blown right back out again." The truth was, the sheriff didn't care. It was a shame, alright; no one denied that. Too bad for the girl. Truth was, she always acted kind of funny, sort of queer, shy and quiet, like she wasn't quite right or something, you know. But it was a shame, alright. A real shame! Still, what's been done can't be undone. And that's the truth of it. Family's no good either. Father's a drunk, mother's a whore. What can you expect? Just the same . . ." and he hawked once or twice, sucked his cheeks and spurted a stream of brown juice through the gap in his big yellow teeth.

When her wounds had healed, her mother ventured out of their shack, humble and apologetic—eager to make amends. Her father stayed in and drank. They ignored the seizures that came in the middle of the night. She could walk. Her eyes weren't swollen. Her bruises were gone. She's alright. Sure, she's alright.

They did not talk about it much. No one in town spoke of it and when she approached, they turned their heads and lowered their eyes, though some slinked away and sniggered together in corners: "Did you know that she ...?" they whispered. But that was all she could hear.

She hurried to the church, stumbling across hills of dirt, losing her shoe and frantically retrieving it.

"Father Jorgé!" She fell at the hem of the priest's black robes.

"A proper confession, now, Carmelita. Nothing less will do."

BLESS ME FATHER FOR I HAVE SINNED.

"Sin of fornication. Don't tell me you don't understand that, Carmelita. That would be lying and that's a sin as well, a grievous one. Now make a good Act of Contrition and be quick about it."

OH, MY GOD, I AM HEARTILY SORRY FOR HAVING OFFENDED THEE...

"What on earth did you do to provoke such an attack, eh, Carmelita? A man is only a man."

What did she do? She must have done something. Something bad, something sinful. It was clear by the look on Father Jorgé's face at morning Mass and by his hand which held the Host and hesitated, always hesitated, as he slipped the white disc on her tongue. She was sinful. And her sin grew in spite of each day's penance, covering up the truth like the swirling red dirt which covered everything.

And the child grew. After four months, even an ignorant peasant girl would have suspected — she was pregnant. It was not that uncommon, not in this forsaken, lonely town. Still, she left without a word to anyone — left the town and the scorn and hitch-hiked one dry, red Saturday a hundred miles to the south, near the border and had the baby in a shriveled-up convent.

LAMB OF GOD, WHO TAKES AWAY THE SINS OF THE WORLD . . .

She crosses herself and kneels. The chains cut into her ankles.

Carmelita . . . is . . . a

"Shhhh." She looks around to find the voices, then bows her grey head, her lips moving feverishly . . . murderer, murderer . . .

The baby never judged, never condemned, when she kissed his tiny pink mouth, stood back and smiled at his gurgling laughter, when she blew a kiss and waved her fingers, holding the pillow behind her back as though they were playing a game, then covered his tiny face with it, holding it down, down, until the little hands and feet stopped jerking. He did not judge. She sat for hours rocking the lifeless form, her breasts filling and dripping his next meal and then she carried him to the church, to the altar and laid him there.

PRAY, BRETHREN, THAT MY SACRIFICE AND YOURS MAY BECOME ACCEPTABLE TO GOD THE FATHER ALMIGHTY.

They found her the next morning, kneeling before the altar, before the cold white body of the child.

SANCTUS. SANCTUS. SANCTUS. . . . murderer . . . murderer . . . murderer.

The bell rings three times. She thumps her breast and squints through the dimness for the voices. She sees nothing but the steely eyes of the matron.

FOR THIS IS MY BODY. My body, my body, she remembers.

MY LORD AND MY GOD.

She raises her eyes to the Host and makes the sign of the cross. Her hands are taken and crossed behind her and she hears the click of the metal cuffs and feels the blood wet in her palms. She is helped to the aisle by the matron. It takes time, as her feet are weighted with shackles. She sees the baby's blood and hers mingled together in the Chalice.

FOR THIS IS MY BODY, she screams.

They gagged her and tied her hands behind her back, pushing her hard against the cold stone floor. The first one was fat and foul-smelling. The second . . .

The priest opens his hands and blesses the congregation.

THE MASS HAS ENDED. GO IN PEACE.

• • •

Sure

Jean Esteve

The sun that succumbed to the mudflats
some time around four in midwinter
was blue as an owl and now its power
to rouse us is gone, gone, like the nuclear
end-of-the-world. I'm glad you were sure.

The sure blue owl circled an earth
mouse-less as your mother's kitchen.
Moon-colored claws cupped the night air
angry and hungry. I'm glad.

Pure truth rose from the mudflats
rusted and covered with barnacles.
There you were with binoculars, shifting your view
from it to owl, from owl to it. I'm glad of your witness,
glad you were sure.

Late Snow

Jean Esteve

In the space of all possible designs,
a particular day, a particular season,
June, and Thursday, in fact,
after morning bloomed gray and noon passed
in stupid silence, toward three
the snow fell, a glance of white
that blossomed once on phlox and yellow roses,
melted then, and disappeared.

Friday sunlight brought us back out to our gardens,
gloved in cotton, nerved with spades and shears,
while out there in the wilderness a desert pelican
rummaged in the dust of ancient ruins.

Snow and Starlight

Jean Esteve

As if snow would cover it.
As if the clouds up there
were tender, protective, a mother polar bear
lumbering to earth to warm her cubs

and I not avid for their fur.
As if there were protection from the snow.

As if stars were friendly,
lighting me to landfall, to a christchild,
grateful for the mercy, lost in night,
while angels round crouch to their errand,
sewing burial robes of whitest cloth.

Then so fierce is my want that I shall wear them,
observing fashion that I never liked nor understood,
as if the fallen snow were meant to warm me,
as if the stars knew where the starlight led.

A Declaration of Faith

Jean Esteve, Waldport, Oregon

Where prayers are effective,
springs gush forth and sequined fishes
swim over sand. Where crying works,
fishes swim over the sand to paupers, handing out hooks,
where crying works and prayers are heard.

Where Americans care
and drive to their fellowships,
trees shoot up out of slash to protect them
shading them gently. Gently shaded
from cancerous sunlight, new possums are born
from tire treads, where Americans care.

When we meet together
to sing holding hands in a circle
fish-full streetpeople leap from the shadows to join us
and sweet baby possums play at our feet.

A Cross-Continental Echo of Faith

Patricia Ranzoni, Bucksport, Maine

Are you saying that all the springs bubbling up, up and
down Maine,
prove that prayers work, even absent sequined fish
swimming on sand?
That if we just cry enough they would swim right over our
shores
to the poor, delivering fish hooks? Then shall we pray?
And cry?

You declare that where Americans care, and wheel to
fellowships to say so,
(Blue Hill Peace & Justice, for example) these shade trees
will spring up
to protect against cancer and the tire tracks we leave will
serve
for animal babies to be born in. Oh, thank you for your
dream!

That when we come together to join hands and candles in
circle, singing,
our homeless and hungry, warm and filled with fish, will
dare appear
and reach back, fuzzy and downy newborns playing at our
feet.
Let us pray, and cry, to believe this.

*In appreciation for Jean Esteve's "A Declaration of Faith"
from her collection,* The Winter Sun *(Turnstone Books of
Oregon, 2013).*

● ● ●
75

Blackberry Air
– after "August" by Mary Oliver

Patricia Ranzoni

And if your ninety-some Augusts
    leaving you with skin thinner
        than a cocoon
            you feel about to flutter from

deem your thorn days done
    but for the memory of their juice, elegant
        on your happy tongue,
            wild,

then may your son, returning
    to the brambles, beyond
        the lady's slippers' song,
            sense your longing

        and reach for you.

Our Own Woman Bear Legend

Patricia Ranzoni

after encountering Alaskan painter, Rie Munoz's 1985 water
base painting at Oceanic Arts in Newport, Oregon, missing
the Naming Ceremony of Sherri L. Mitchell of the Penobscot
Nation in Maine

We who love her, the young woman running barefoot in
the ferns
through the wooded cover, her skirt aswirl, arms spread
high in flight,
blueberries hailing through her flying fingers and hair
from her upflung basket know
it isn't the massive black bear turning to her just a nuzzle
away
causing her fright. Oh, no, that would be her clan
gathering near
to be present when the berries bounce and roll under the
leaves,
over the moss, between the stones, showing her paths
to other mysteries of her nature, the new Spirit Name
she is being led to ~ maybe with an aspect representing
that she is of the longest, strongest river in her land,
the serpentine Penobscot of the dawn side.

We who love her send this blessing from around earth ~
that her ash basket forever spill fruits capable
of seeding stories with the power to transform fear into
food,
earning the old name her elders will bestow, knowing.

We who love her, laugh, seeing our own legend so
surprised.

ONE BY ONE BY DRONE
OR
YOU PRAY I'LL SEW

Patricia Ranzoni

pantoum variation

As if it will do any good,
all you who stitch –
Nickulas, Leon and Gal, Cheryl, Peter, Jude,
take up your needles and threads.

All you who stitch,
make squares! Protest your best!
Take up your needles and threads to
join quilts tough enough to block drones.

Make squares! Protest your best!
Fortify with more than tears.
Join quilts tough enough to block drones.
Save a child! With his name. Age.

Fortifying with more than tears,
create a tapestry of your grief,
saving a child with her name and age,
remaking outrage into testimony.

Craft tapestry of your grief, I say.
By love can we save our failing hearts
remaking outrage into testimony,
for example, this boy assigned to me?

With love can we save our failing hearts
before we die,
for example, this boy assigned to me?
This boy playing on his family's Gaza roof.

Before we die,
tell the truth
about the children targeted on their family roof
some say died some that's a lie.

Tell the truth!
No excuse! Child flesh is child flesh. Blood blood.
Some say he died some that's a lie.
Little cubic wounds are little cubic wounds.

No excuse! Child flesh is child flesh. Blood blood.
Choice not to divert, children or not. *Stitch! Stitch! Sew!*
Little cubic wounds little cubic wounds.
(Whisper *traps traps! Joy sticks joy sticks . . . .*)

Choice not to divert, children or not. *Stitch! Stitch! Sew!*
See his appliquéd kite from my calico stash?
(Whisper *traps, traps! Joy sticks, joy sticks . . . .*)
My many-colored floss knots guiding its tail?

See his appliquéd kite from my calico stash
sailing up through his family's exploding lunch?
My many-colored floss knots guiding its tail?
His brief life rising to the heavens his baby brother?

Sailing up through his family's exploding lunch
a beloved boy's soul going. (*Mother!*)
His brief life rising to the heavens his baby brother
(*Sister!*) sewn on a fiber artist's hand-dyed tumult.

A beloved son's soul going. (*Father!*)
through the drone-strike smoke and white dust
(*Sister!*) shown by a fiber artist's hand-dyed tumult.
His see-through hand. His name. Yours.

_ _

Oh sew to the Creator of Fibers and Conceivers
threading Will into being, especially children
who shall not come again,
that by doing this excruciatingly insufficient thing

we might believe it will do some, however slight, good.

AUTHORS

Orpha Barry--world traveler, writer of plays and poems, still searches for answers to unanswerable questions, while tossing pebbles into the sea.

Sandra Ellston keeps trying to retire from a forty-year career as a professor of Shakespeare, poetry, film, and theory. She is author of numerous poems and articles in journals, notably "Hearing Ophelia," as well as *Econolingua* and *Poems Along the Way*. She serves as President of Writers on the Edge and is founder and organizer of the Northwest Poets' Concord. She currently is at work on memoirs and film noir and various editing projects.

Jean Esteve is a Waldport poet. Her chapbook, "Off-Key," published by Finishing Line Press, was a 2013 finalist for the Oregon Book Award. A new collection, "The Winter Sun," was released by Turnstone Books of Oregon in 2013.

Brian Hanna was born in Ireland. From the time he was a toddler he enjoyed playing with words. "We were too poor to buy toys, but words are cheap," he explains. He considered careers in law and on the stage but abandoned the law on discovering it wasn't just about eloquence and swanning around in a wig. Stage ambitions were, he admits, quickly abandoned for precisely the same reasons. For most of his working life he has been an architect in Canada. Now he mostly writes comedy pieces. It doesn't make any money, but it doesn't cost that much either. The outlays on writing seminars and self-publishing are, he imagines, modest, when compared to the costs of keeping a mistress or a time share in the Virgin Islands.

Ruth F. Harrison is a retired professor of medieval literature. Publications include two textbooks, four poetry collections (*Bone Flute*, 1996; *Namesong* , 2004; *How Singular and Fine*, a collection of formal poetry, 2012); and *West of 101* (2013); three chapbooks; poems included in Turco's *The Book of Forms* (2012) and in *The Lyric*'s children's anthology (2012). Her recent work appears in *Harp Strings, Kestrel, Denver Quarterly, Plainsong, The Lyric, Trinacria*, and many other journals, and in the Oregon bridges anthology; and online in *packratnest* and Lewis Turco's blog. Her poems have won numerous awards in *Formalist,* NFSPS, and OPA (OSPA) contests. She has just been awarded a lifetime membership in OPA.

Cynthia Jacobi Being a visual artist as well as a poet, I often find that one enhances the other. I live on the Oregon coast with endless prompts from nature. One of my goals in life is, in the words of William Stafford, "to be awake."

Donny King is a west coast singer and songwriter who plays a B.B. King Cadillac guitar.

Sue McGhee has been writing since the age of twelve. Her first novel, "When the Eagle Flies with the Condor," was published in 2011. She has a BA in English from the University of Colorado and studied for her MA at Portland State University. In 2002, she published a collection of short stories entitled "Voices" and is now editing her own collection of literary essays soon to be published. Sue and her husband, Dave, recently moved from Colorado and now live on the central Oregon coast.

Crystal McGuire is an Alaskan-born poet of Native American descent who works as a media specialist and lives with her husband and two sons in Toledo.

Shirley Plummer is a native Oregonian poet currently recovering from a year of illness and accident. She is

• • •

starting slowly with revisions, forms that require shared authorship, and lots of reading.

Patricia Ranzoni's work has been published across the country and abroad, including previous issues of the TUESDAY anthology, having participated with the group for a decade. Home is with family on the Maine and Oregon coasts. In 2013 she was nominated for a St. Botolph Foundation Emerging Artist Award. Her ninth book, *FLIGHTS & GLORIES, Poems Between the Atlantic & Pacific,* will be published by Turnstone Books of Oregon.

Kathleen Sullivan was a Roman Catholic nun, a teacher, a social worker, and an attorney. She now lives on the Oregon coast where she fishes, crabs, gardens, and writes. Her novel, *What the Dog Dug Up,* a humorous mystery, was published in 2004.